D0646183

ISBN 978-0-9802439-0-1

Library of Congress Control Number 2007943220

Copyright © 2008

Published by *catersource llc*
250 Marquette Avenue South, Suite 550, Minneaplis, MN 55401
To order: 877.932.3632 or www.catersource.com

Printed in the USA

Cover & book design by Jean Blackmer

IF YOU DON'T SELL IT YOU CAN'T COOK IT

MICHAEL ROMAN

catersource®
MAGAZINE, CONFERENCE & TRADESHOW

INTRODUCTION

This book offers catering salespeople the resources to do their jobs better. Inside, you will find checklists, guides, tips, strategies and, most important, scripts that will help you excel and raise your closing average. The book doesn't really have a beginning or end; it is, first and foremost, a resource guide designed to help catering salespeople sharpen their skills and fulfill their goals.

Here are some numbers that will help put selling in perspective. Out of every ten potential clients you attempt to sell:

- Three won't buy from you no matter what you do or don't do. They just don't like you or feel comfortable with you. You may be too tall or short, old or young … whatever. It really isn't your fault; it's just the nature of people and how they purchase goods and services.

- Another three will buy from you no matter what you do or don't do! They like you and/or your company's reputation.

- The remaining four come looking for a caterer with an open mind. They are going to buy catering from someone and soon. These shoppers are trying to figure out how catering and caterers work. They are in search of value, quality and leadership to help them through the maze of decisions they need to make in order to have a successful event. This book will help you make these four shoppers select you over your competitors.

Some may be born salespeople, but with knowledge and practice, anyone can become a sales winner. Selling is the art of making friends in a short amount of time. This book sums up most of what I have learned, discovered or created while training salespeople over the last four decades.

The simple truth—which is not clearly understood by many catering businesses—is that the catering salesperson is the catalyst of all company growth. If the salespeople don't sell it, the chefs can't cook it, the staff can't serve it and the guests can't enjoy it and ask the client "Who did your catering?"

There are no tricks or short cuts to better sales—just practice. Selling catering is fun, rewarding, and filled with excitement — especially if you are prepared.

Michael Roman
Catersource President and Founder
mikeroman@catersource.com

USING SCRIPTS

Successful salespeople have one thing in common: They don't wing it or make up their selling presentations as they go. They create and then test a series of scripts that help them stay on track. These scripts are very much like those an actor uses on the stage or in a movie.

Like an actor, a salesperson needs to memorize and rehearse the scripts, then use them in real selling situations to verify their effectiveness with prospects. If they help win sales, the scripts are kept in the "performance." If they don't bring positive results, they are reworked or replaced. This cycle of practicing, adjusting and confirming is a constant with winning salespeople.

A successful salesperson doing three sales presentations to three different prospects on the same day, will say exactly the same things to each one. Each prospect will hear the same opening, questions and closing that the others heard. This discipline and repetition is the cornerstone of greater sales success.

Think of your scripts as a recipe for victory. Chefs, after perfecting a recipe, follow it to the letter to insure continued success. So, too, should a salesperson follow proven scripts.

As you go through the book, you'll realize that there is too much for one salesperson to use all at once. That's not a problem. Select two or three scripts from each section to create your own selling performance. You may find it helpful to transfer your favorite scripts to index cards, so you can study and rehearse them easily.

TABLE OF CONTENTS

FUNDAMENTALS

What does a salesperson do? What do potential customers for catering want from the salesperson—and what are they concerned about?

Understanding the hopes, dreams and expectations of each party to a sale—the buyer and the salesperson—is important to making the sales process work.

What does a salesperson do?

A good salesperson is a combination of a lawyer, a psychologist, a coach, an accountant, an entertainer and a good friend. Charm is important, but it's not even close to being enough. A good salesperson has to have the goods, as well as the personality. A salesperson:

- Speaks clearly and precisely at all times, particularly during a selling interview.

- Answers typical buyer objections before they come up.

- Plans sales calls in advance and makes a sales plan for each day.

- Decides ahead of time what to sell to the buyer.

- Asks good, probing questions.

- Is always honest in the approach to selling.

- Uses sales aids while selling. Involves all of the buyers' senses: hearing, sight, smell, touch and taste.

- Sells the concept that the catering will never embarrass the buyer in front of friends, family or coworkers.

- Takes the risk out of buying when possible.

- Uses time properly. Isn't afraid to stop a "going nowhere" selling presentation to move on to a better prospect.

- Listens to the meaning of what the buyer is saying, not just the words.

- Acts professional at all times.

- Never apologizes for the price; explains what the price guarantees for the buyer.

- If the sale is missed, understands why and doesn't take it personally.

- Is in constant search of competitor data.

- Is ready to sell 24 hours a day.

- Isn't afraid of making mistakes or trying new selling techniques.

What do buyers want a salesperson to do?

Buyers have their own ideas about what a salesperson will do in their interaction. They feel good about—and are more likely to buy from—a salesperson who meets or exceeds their expectations. They expect you to:

- tell them the truth.

- listen to them.

- take them seriously.

- give clear explanations.

- make them feel important.

- avoid embarrassing them.

- make them part of the process.

- meet their personal and professional goals.

- help them work less, not more.

- take the blame for anything that goes wrong.

- help them be recognized by their peers.

- help them get promoted.

- help them avoid any pain or discomfort in planning an event.

- like them and to consider them fair.

- give them the best price.

- help them understand what caterers do.

- take the risks out of their planning.

What are the buyers' motives?

Buyers may have several motives for planning an event and for working with the catering team. These affect what the buyer may want from the caterer and how the sales process is conducted. Possible motives include:

- **Achievement.** Having a successful event will show others what they've been able to accomplish.

- **Independence.** A recently divorced person, for example, may give a party to establish his or her new status to peers.

- **Exhibition.** This party will be better than the last party.

- **Recognition.** A parent gives a graduation party or a bar mitzvah.

- **Dominance.** The buyer may need to be in total control of the situation.

- **Affiliation.** A buyer wants your name on the event, which puts the buyer in the same league as peers.

- **Charity.** This buyer wants to use the event to raise money for a worthy cause.

- **Self-fulfillment.** The buyer sees the event as a way to show how forward-thinking he or she is (and may need to be told that).

- **Romance.** The buyer is concerned about the look and feel of the event, including the theme and appearance of the staff, and about the happiness of the guests.

- **Education.** The buyer has the Martha Stewart Complex and wants to learn everything he or she can about how you put together a catered event.

A salesperson's checklist

Check your own progress—and do it often—with the answers to these questions. If you answer "no" to any questions, there's work for you to do to be more effective.

- Are you getting the sales volume you should?

- Do you know how many sales your company expects of you this year?

- Do you always talk to the right person when selling catering?

- Do you have a consistent and proven sales script for qualifying the caller?

- Do you spend too much time with clients who really can't buy?

- Do you spend at least two days a week out of the office prospecting for customers?

- Do you know how much one of your work hours is worth in dollars?

- Have you set a three-year income goal for yourself?

- Have you read at least three books on selling in the last year?

- Do you keep your past sales figures handy so you can review them quickly?

- Have you spent time analyzing your competitors?

- Do you talk with other sales people or managers at your company about your sales efforts?

- Do you know what your closing average is?

- Do you keep records on what takes place during each sales call?

- During the last month, have you talked to the chef about the menu items you sell?

- Are you eating lunch once a week at an association or community event of some kind?

- When you know you're going to an area to make a confirmed call, do you prospect for other potential clients?

- Do you know which factors make selling catering difficult?

- Are you pro-active about selling your company?

- Are you having fun when you sell?

The path to a sale

Every sale is different, of course, but the same basic process should be followed. These steps can lead you to a successful sales experience.

- Be pleasant and remember to smile as you speak or listen either in person or when talking over the phone. Your first sale is to make them look upon you as a business friend.

- Qualify the shopper before you begin your sales presentation.

- Take notes as the shopper speaks and refer to your prepared notes along the way to stay on course.

- Answer or neutralize any and all objections before moving forward.

- Ask a variety of scripted questions to gain insight into the worries and joys of the shopper.

- Engage everyone in front of you during the sales presentation.

- Explain how the shopper reserves their date, all the costs and how the deposit policy works before or during your close.

- Continue to smile and demonstrate leadership.

- Answer all the shopper's questions with another question that relates to the close.

- If your first choice close doesn't work or gets bogged down, ease up and restate why your company is the right choice for their catering. Get the shopper's confirmation on your advantages and close again.

• When the sale is made, embrace them
  with your congratulations and
  appreciation. You have made a new
  business friend. Now the upsell begins.

Remember: Shoppers can buy catering from lots of different companies, but they can only get you if they purchase from your company. Brochures, videos, websites and lower prices don't make sales happen. You make sales happen. Catering buyers decide on which company to select based on how much they like and trust the salesperson. It's really that simple.

QUALIFYING

The first step in the sales process is figuring out how likely a potential customer is to become a client. Is your company right for the customer? Is the timing going to be right? Do the economics make sense?

You don't want to spend more time than you have to dealing with people who aren't likely to buy your catering services. How do you determine quickly and politely whether this potential customer qualifies?

In the script, pay particular attention to the phrases that are in bold; these are the keys to helping the customer understand the process.

General qualification

Both you and the potential client need very basic information to start, such as whether your services are available on the day the client's event is planned. This basic script is for the first telephone contact with a potential client.

"ABC Catering, may we help you?"

Caller: I'd like to get some information about your catering?

"Thanks for calling. My name is Ted. If I may ask you just a few questions, I'll be able to serve you better or place you with the right person. Please tell me, what date you are you looking to reserve for your catering?"

Caller: June 25

"For approximately how many guests?"

Caller: About 125 guests

"And what type of event will it be?"

Caller: A wedding.

"Is June 25 your primary date selection or do you have an alternative date also?"

Caller: No, June 25 is the day we need.

"Thank you. Please let me check our reservation book to make sure that June 25 is still available for your wedding of 125 guests. May I place you on hold?"

Even if you know that the date that the caller wishes is wide open, you still need to place them on hold to establish the fact that you are a "hot" and busy company.

"Thank you for waiting. Yes, I'm happy to say that June 25 is still available. May I please have your name?"

Notice that only now are we asking the caller for their name. It is unwise to ask the caller their name immediately after answering the phone because you have a chance of losing control if the caller hesitates to give you their name and instead asks a question like "How much does a wedding cost?" Now you are off on a caller-driven tangent before you have the basic info about their needs.

Caller: Sarah Weaver

"Okay Sarah, from what you've told me so far I'm convinced that you should be speaking with Mary Stevens, our sales manager. Mary specializes in weddings. I'll get her for you right away. [or: Mary is with another client at the moment. May I have her call you later today?]"

[Mary Stevens talks to customer]

"Hello, Ms. Weaver, Ted tells me that you are planning a wedding for 125 guests on June 25. Have you ever been to one of our catered events?"

- [If the answer is no]

"Let me tell you a little about our company ..."

- [If the answer is yes]

I guess you already know ...

Questions on the buyer's mind

The client is trying to determine whether you're the right caterer for the event—and whether they feel comfortable with you. Remember that many potential customers may not have used a caterer before and don't know how to work with one. These kinds of questions may go through their minds:

- Will I be able to participate in the planning?

- How much extra food do they send?

- Will they ask me difficult questions?

- What does the staff look like?

- Will I be embarrassed in front of my guests?

- Is the food good?

- Will they run out of food during my event?

- What will it cost me?

- Is the price fair?

- Will they show-up on time?

- Is their kitchen clean?

- Has anyone gotten ill eating their food?

- Will they still be in business on party day?

- Who else has bought from them?

- What things could go wrong?

- How will our place look after they leave?

Taking these questions and using the script to qualify the caller would result in the following:

"Let me tell you a little about our company. As a leading caterer in (city), we pride ourselves in offering outstanding food and professionally trained service staff that will create an event to please your guest and eliminate any chance of embarrassment. We encourage our clients to make us aware of any and all wishes they have while planning the event. Our culinary staff practices the highest level of sanitation and always prepares ample amounts of food at very fair prices. Some of our happy clients who have given us permission to mention their names are ... "

(Notice how many of the questions you've already answered for the caller without them even asking.)

Telling the price of admission

How do you and the potential client figure out whether you're in the same price range? Often, callers are obsessed with asking "How much does your catering cost?" during the first ten seconds of the call.

When the question of cost comes up, use this script:

"We have a wonderful variety of wedding menus [packages] that range from $65 to $125 per guest, depending on the day of the week, the menu you select and the style of service you wish. Is that the range you were looking for?"

In an attempt to take control, the caller may tell you flatly that they have a specific price already in mind. Use a variation of these scripts to respond:

"$18 is a great place to start. Please tell me what your budget is on the higher end."

"I realize that you wish to learn about our $18 per guest menus, but I was also hoping to show you some menus that are a little lower. Would that be alright with you? (They always answer yes.) Good. Besides the lower cost menus, I will also show you a few that are slightly higher in price."

Did you sense that in this script when you say to the prospect "but I was also hoping to show you some menus that are a little lower" that they were expecting you to say "higher" instead of "lower?" Try to do some unexpected things when using scripts.

BEGINNING THE SALE

Opening the sales process, you want to present information about your catering in the most positive light—and to make sure that you are answering the questions the client needs or should need to make decisions.

The scripts in this section help the customer get to know you and your company, and demonstrate your interest in them—an important factor in their deciding to use your company and in their satisfaction with your services. Everyone wants to feel as if they are understood and appreciated and maybe loved.

Preparing to sell a potential client

Before you make your scripted and rehearsed presentation to a potential client, you need to be prepared. That means not only having the information you need about your company, but also understanding what motivates the buyer and how you will act during the selling process. Know the answers to these questions:

- Why will my catering and my company benefit this customer?

- What will the customer lose if he or she buys from someone else?

- Is the person I'll be meeting with today the one who has the power to purchase from me?

- Am I ready to tell the customer about the benefits of my company in specific detail?

- Do I have evidence (testimonials) to back up my beliefs in my product and services?

- Will I remember to listen to the meaning of what the customer says?

- Will I be able to answer questions without any hesitation?

- How am I going to react to the customer's first objection? To the second?

- Do I have a set of prepared questions to draw out the buyer's thoughts and beliefs?

- What am I going to do if the customer says "maybe"? If the customer says "no"?

- Am I prepared to place my ego on the line?

- Am I ready to ask for the order or appointment? Do I know what close I might use?

- How many times am I going to ask for the order or appointment?

- Can I talk knowledgeably about the competition?

- Am I ready to ask for help selling from my peers and managers?

Opening scripts

Your first meeting with the client may be at the client's home or office, or at your own facility. These opening scripts help the client feel comfortable with you, and allow both you and the client to get a sense about how you might work together. Choose the opening scripts that make the most sense for you.

"I'm sure that you will be pleased to know that we still have openings on the day you're planning to hold your event."

"If you're interested in having a beautiful catered event at the best value, then you will enjoy the information I'm going to give you."

"Everyone around here seems so happy and in high spirits ... what's your secret for keeping them so motivated?"
[If you are at the client's office]

"What is it you like most about your work?"

"It's really difficult for me to describe the benefits of the room I have available for your upcoming wedding; you really have to see it. I suggest we get you here as soon as possible because the date you've chosen is a very popular one. I'd like to be the one who shows you the space. Are you able to meet with me at 7:00 p.m. Wednesday, or would 3:00 p.m. Saturday be better?"

"I'm sure you've given this event a lot of thought. What are some of the items on your wish list for the event? What will make it a success for you?"

"To make best use of our time together today, do you mind if I ask you a few questions first?"

"Before we begin today, I'd like to tell you why I decided to join the sales team at ABC Catering.

"Before we begin, I'd like to tell you about a great event we did last week."

"Before we begin, I'd like to ask whether you would like me to give you in-depth information about our catering, or a shorter version that will let us get to the menu selections and price sooner. Which would you like?"

Tip

Could you use this script?
> *"Before we begin, may I ask if you've already decided to use our company for your event?"*

It takes a certain amount of courage — and you have to do it honestly and with integrity.

If they infer they are looking at other companies, then you might wish to use this script:
> *"Which other companies are you looking at? I might be able to give you tips on them."*

INFORMATION

The sales conversation is an exchange of information back and forth. You're telling customers the information they need to know to make a decision about which caterer to choose and what options they have for the event. At the same time, you're getting information that tells you what kind of client this is, what you need to do to make a sale—and to put on the event they want.

It's easy to get so absorbed in the conversation that you forget to get some of the information you need. Before sitting down with a client, make a checklist of the questions you need to have the client answer, so you won't forget anything.

The basics

Who, what, why, when ... don't forget the basic questions you need to put together a proposal:

"When is the event?"

"How many people are expected?"

"What is the reason for the event?"

"Do you have an alternate date?"

"Have you done this event before?"

"Who catered this event last time?"

"Which caterers have you used in the past?"

"What other catering companies are you considering?"

"How much time will you need before you choose your caterer?"

"What colors do you like best?"

"Will there be any speakers at the event?"

"What will your schedule be during the event?"

"At what time will you need access to our banquet room for your decorations?"

"When do you expect the event to end?"

"Will you need any special help after your guests leave?"

These questions are a lot to memorize. It is perfectly proper for a salesperson to use notes while presenting information. By having this "cheat sheet," your confidence and ability can increase dramatically. Simply say:

"You will notice that I refer to my yellow pad to make sure I stay on track while getting all the important information I need to make your event a huge success. I do this because I get so excited about what I do that I sometimes forget to ask something."

Getting more specific

You may need more specifics from the client in order to understand what the expectations for the event are:

"I hope I'm not imposing on you, but could you answer a few questions for me so I can put together the best possible proposal?"

"I must be kind of slow today. Could you go over that one more time, please?"

"How will our catering help your company sell its products?"

"What would be your dream event?"

"Parties are very special events. How often do you throw a party?"

"Where do you see the differences between other caterers' proposals and ours?"

"Cost aside, which of these menus do you like most?"

"Just between you and me, is there anything we can do to get you to become a customer?"

"So, you're saying that if I can get our manager to approve a lower deposit you could become a customer?"

"Can you give me an example of what you mean?"

"I remember you telling me that your budget is limited. What exactly do you mean by 'limited.'"

Clarifying expectations

Just because the customer is sitting in front of you, doesn't mean he or she will be in charge of making decisions about this event. It's important to understand what the customer's expectations are, and how different parties involved with the event (family of the bride, the customer's manager, etc.) will interact. Questions like these can help:

"Who, besides you, is going to be involved in the decision of which caterer you use?"

"Who should I send a copy of the menus and other information to?" (This tips you off to who else is important in the decision)

"What is your expectation on the time for me to get my information back to you?" (If you hear the words, "There's no rush," pack up and leave).

"Ideally, when would you be ready to make a decision about which caterer you will use?"

"What are your expectations for this event?"

"What is your experience in dealing with your boss? What menu is likely to appeal to her?"

"You don't seem to be as concerned about the number of service staff as you are about the service charges. Am I right about that? What are you thinking?"

"Have you had much experience in purchasing catering?"

"You seem very pleased. Is there anything I can do to make you even happier?"

"You seem to be holding something back … what is it?"

"Most of the people I work with don't seem to be in such a rush to get the information. Is there a reason you want to move quickly?"

"Do you know any reason your husband wouldn't like what we've put together today?"

"What were the highlights of your last catered event?"

"When you first glanced at this menu, what caught your eye?"

"You expressed an interest in fewer staff. What are you looking for in terms of staff?"

Offering more

Although you're asking the client for information, you're also giving information about how your company offers them the tools to have a successful event:

"Many of my clients like me to bring them up to date on the latest food trends. Would you like me to take a moment and do this?"

"I find that some clients wish to serve a dessert at the table followed by a surprise Viennese dessert buffet. Would you like to surprise your guests?"

"It's important to me that the numbers on your proposal are done the way you want to review them. Do you prefer the costs to be wrapped up all in one number, or do you want to have them broken down into separate costs?"

"Alex is one of our finest maitre d's; do you wish to reserve him for your event?"

"I seem to do better after I understand what my clients are thinking of doing during the event. Would you please take a moment and let me know your thoughts?"

"Sales meetings can be fun. Would you like me to explain how this can be done?"

"I have no idea if this will appeal to you, but have you ever thought of doing a buffet instead of plate service?"

"Can you imagine how happy your guests will be when they see the dessert tables being rolled out?"

"It's amazing how many people don't like to pay for valet parking. Do you think that our paid parking passes will make them happier?"

"Guests usually expect special foods at a wedding. What types of food do you like?"

"I realize that when planning an event the host likes to have constant contact with the catering company. Would you like to have my cell number just in case?"

"I find that the way a facility's lobby impacts a guest is very important. Did you find our lobby as beautiful as I do?"

Questions using attitude

Remember to appeal to the customer's feelings, even for some of the most basic information. Don't ask "How many serving staff do you want?" Instead, ask, "What are your feelings about the number of serving staff?" The following questions are examples of how you can appeal to the emotions:

"Sarah, what are your feelings about the number of serving staff at the event?"

"Are you concerned about the amount of time it will take for your guests to go through the buffet?"

"Are you leaning towards the premium entreés like a seafood combo, or should I stick with the more traditional ones, like chicken?"

"When figuring our price, do you want me to consider premium liquor?"

"Would you like me to explain our feelings about tipping event staff?"

"What do you think about hors d'oeuvre before the dinner?"

"How do you feel about valet parking?"

"I sense that you are a little unsure about this. Why is that?"

When speaking to multiple buyers at the same time, be sure to square your body with the person you're directing your question to. Don't just move your head in the direction of a person sitting to the left if you are addressing them; move your entire body towards them to show your interest in their question or response.

ENHANCING

The way you conduct the sales discussion can enhance the customer's sense of confidence in your company—and the sale itself. Certain words and phrases invite the customer's involvement, and that's likely to lead to a more successful outcome for everyone involved.

The words and phrases in this section can be combined with many requests for information from the client or statements about your catering services. Notice how they don't just address the customer; they invite the customer.

Powerful selling phrases

The following scripts for starting a sentence are simple, but important. They enhance the image of your catering company and set you apart from your competitors with just a word or two.

"Unlike other caterers ..."

"At ABC Catering, we ..."

"Very few caterers have ..."

"Our clients tell us that ..."

"One reason for our success is ..."

"A great event depends on ..."

"It takes a special team of people to ..."

Sense the sales impact when using these phrases:

Our menus are customized **vs**
*"Unlike other caterers our menus
are customized."*

We send 10 percent additional food **vs**
*"At ABC Catering we send 10 percent
additional food."*

We have a staff training program **vs**
*"Very few caterers have a staff
training program."*

We have outstanding food **vs**
*"Our clients tell us that we have
outstanding food."*

We develop creative menus **vs**
*"One reason for our success is
we develop creative menus."*

Long lines are wrong **vs**
*"Remember, we don't want to
have long lines."*

Correct planning is important **vs**
*"A great event depends on
correct planning."*

Our catering team is great **vs**
*"It takes a special team of people
to create great events."*

Exciting words

Words matter. Use strong descriptive words as often as possible to make sure the customer has a sense of the quality of your catering and to appeal to the atmosphere the customer wants for the event. This list is helpful; find the powerful words that work best for you. Remember, nouns don't make sales: Verbs, adjectives and adverbs make sales.

- Accessible
- Acclaimed
- Accomplishes
- Affordable
- Alluring
- Bold

- Breathtaking
- Capable
- Carefree
- Casual
- Celebrated
- Changed

- Chic
- Clarifies
- Classic
- Clear
- Comprehensive
- Countless
- Critical
- Crucial
- Current
- Dynamic
- Elegant
- Elegant
- Elite
- Enlightening
- Essential

- Essential
- Excellence
- Exclusive
- Exhaustive
- Expanded
- Explosive
- Extensive
- Famous
- Fascinating
- Fast
- Favorite
- Festive
- Finesse
- Flexible
- Foolproof

- Futuristic
- Genuine
- Glowing
- Handy
- Harmony
- Heady
- Immense
- Imperative
- Important
- Inexpensive
- Ingenious
- Integrity
- Intricate
- Invaluable
- Irresistible

- Legendary
- Lively
- Magical
- Magnificent
- Major
- Masterpiece
- Matchless
- Memorable
- Modern
- Natural
- New
- Outstanding
- Perfected
- Plush
- Posh

- Prestige
- Prestigious
- Prevents
- Profitable
- Prominent
- Proven
- Pure
- Qualified
- Quick
- Real
- Refined
- Relaxed
- Remarkable
- Reorganized
- Reputable

- Respected
- Revealing
- Revered
- Revived
- Revolutionary
- Roomy
- Sassy
- Significant
- Simplified
- Sizzling
- Skilled
- Soothing
- Special
- Spectacular
- Spicy

- Splendid
- Staggering
- Stirring
- Stunning
- Substantial
- Sumptuous
- Superb
- Superior
- Talented
- Tempting
- Thrifty
- Timeless
- Top-drawer
- Unassuming
- Unforgettable

- Unhurried
- Unlimited
- Unprecedented
- Unswerving
- Useful
- Value
- Versatile
- Vital
- Vitality
- Vivid
- Weeping
- Wonderful
- Worthwhile
- Zesty

 Each script is a series of words that create sentences to help you provide shoppers with the information and questions needed to secure the sale. Often, the elimination or addition of a single word can raise or lower the selling power of the script.

OBJECTIONS

Wouldn't it be wonderful if you made your presentation, the customer nodded and bam, you had a sale? It almost never happens like that—nor should it.

Objections are required to make a sale! In fact, the caterer should encourage them and be suspicious when a buyer is not stating any objections; they are the foundation of most sales.

When objections arise, you have an opportunity to determine what really motivates your customer. That means you can do a better job of satisfying the customer by responding to those motivations, concerns and worries

The single biggest reason that buyers give objections is to insulate themselves from having to make a decision—even when they already have decided to buy your catering. In general, most buyers of anything want to hold off until the last moment.

Why customers raise objections

There are many reasons a customer may raise objections. It may be as simple as the customer not understanding something, or as complicated as the customer fearing that he or she can't afford your services, but being embarrassed to say so. Some of the reasons a customer may raise objections are:

- Normal hesitancy.

- Loyalty to their current catering company.

- Fear of making a mistake.

- Not convinced by your sales pitch.

- Don't have the money (objections are a way to avoid embarrassment).

- Have the money, but have other priorities.

- Private.

- Don't like you.

- Don't trust you.

- Being confused (maybe because you didn't present the information clearly).

- You've highlighted the wrong benefits.

- You waited too long for the close.

- You used the wrong examples or "war stories."

- Don't sense your enthusiasm while you're selling.

How to move through objections

You can't ignore objections, hoping they will go away; you need to address them and move on. Here are some tips for handling objections:

Make sure that both you and your buyer understand what the objection is.

"Sarah, I'm not sure I understand what you mean. Are you saying that ... ?"

"Please repeat your last comment. I apologize; I don't think I heard you correctly."

Provide a safe opportunity for your buyer to raise or state an objection.

"Is there anything you need clarification on?"

"Sarah, do you disagree with anything I've talked about?"

"It would help me greatly if you made me aware of any concerns you have about the information I'm presenting today."

Determine if there is a valid objection or if you have a buyer who is nervous about getting close to buying your catering.

"Ms. Weaver, does your concern really have great weight over whether you purchase our catering, or is it something we can fix after we reserve the date for the wedding?"

"That is a valid concern, but I really don't think that will happen. Do you?"

"Let me share with you what one of my clients did to insure that ..."

Try to overcome the objection before it arises.

"Sarah, let me take a few minutes to share with you why I decided, to work for ABC Catering. In this way you will understand why ABC is the top company in town."

Use objections to help move you to the close.

"Sarah, if that answers your concern, which color linen do you wish for the event, the yellow or the light blue?"

Listen to the meaning of the words the buyer uses, not just the words themselves.

"It seems to me, Sarah, that what you're really saying is ..."

Rush towards objections and accept them as your challenge!

"I like the way you put that, Ms. Weaver. What I'd like to do now is to explain how we'll eliminate your concern. Then I'd like to hear about any other concerns you may have."

*"Is this the only concern holding you back?
Suppose we can overcome this problem;
what other concerns would you have?"*

---

*"If cost were no object, what would be
the ideal solution?"*

---

*"What would you like us to do to get past
this concern?"*

---

*"It seems as if you have several valid
concerns. Which would you put in first
place and which would be second in
importance?"*

---

*"I understand you need some time to
think, and I'd like to help you.
What are some of the things you want
to think over?"*

Concerns about price

The biggest hurdle for many customers, especially those who have never worked with a caterer before, is price. They're worried they can't pay what you're asking, or that they will pay more than they should. Here are some answers when the customer says something like "You're so expensive":

"Several clients this week have made the same comment. Let me take a moment and share with you what I told them about being higher priced."

"Yes, but I thought that is exactly why you are here today: You know that we do the best job."

"What would you like to pay for this event?"

"Yes, we are one of the more expensive catering companies in town, but we also have the most clients—so we really must be doing something right."

"Yes, Ms. Weaver, we are expensive, but we stand behind everything we do. You won't have any complaints, mishaps or failures."

"We are very professional, Ms. Weaver, and we really don't expect to sell everyone. We need to charge prices that permit us to maintain the professional staff and high standards of the ABC Catering company."

Stronger concerns about price

The customer may compare your prices to those of other caterers being considered, so the objection is not just that your prices are high, but that they are higher than other caterers. In this case, you need to respond to the comparison as well as to the concern about cost:

"When a caterer doesn't have any track record, they usually offer lower prices, which results in lower levels of experience and quality that foster much more risk for the host."

"Many customers think that all caterers are the same, just as the same model of a car is the same, no matter what dealer you buy it from. But you're not buying a car when you buy catering. Let me explain: If you can decide on a particular car model that you want and then go to

different car dealers and try to get the best price, that's great; a Cadillac is a Cadillac. But when you call and get different prices from different caterers for the same menu, you are buying qualities that you can't examine by "kicking the tires," such as experience, track record, quality of suppliers, cleanliness, staff and the overall investment in the profession. Spending $500 less on a caterer could become one of your worst nightmares, like buying a Cadillac and ending up with a Chevrolet."

"Yes, Ms. Weaver, we realize that we charge more than many caterers in town, but when we started ABC Catering, we quickly realized that we could charge less by giving less, as some other caterers have chosen to do. Or, we could charge a realistic and fair price that would allow us to maintain a catering business that offers only the finest quality in order not to embarrass our clients, their guests or ourselves. So, Ms. Weaver, I'm sure that you want only the best for your friends, don't you?"

"We hear that from many people, and it's an honest comment. But because we charge a little more, we are able to put a lot more into the order. So, I think the extra money is worth your peace of mind because you won't have to worry about the success of the party. What do you think?"

"As you know, as with most things that you buy, you get what you pay for."

"Since you brought up XYZ Catering, let me share with you some of the major and minor differences between the two of us ..."

"Yes, XYZ is somewhat cheaper than we are, but look over this list of clients who have switched to us from XYZ because of what they discovered after they tried us just once."

When the customer has a specific comparison, such as: "But, I can get the chicken dinners from down the street for a dollar less."

"Ms. Weaver, if you really want to try us I'll guarantee your dollar difference back to you. If you honestly believe that you and your guests aren't happier with our chicken dinners I'll refund you the difference in price between theirs and ours."

"What would you say to me if I told you that I would sell you the chicken dinners at exactly the same price as down the street if you let me buy the chicken I use for your dinners from his supplier rather than mine and if you will let me give you the same portions of food he gives rather than our portions?"

Above all, never apologize about having higher prices. Never. Simply start with an admission of truth and explain what the buyer gets from your company over the others.

Concerns about your company

The customer may be concerned about your company in particular, based on an experience someone else has had, a rumor about your company—or perhaps their own experience in the past. Or the customer may have had a bad experience with another caterer and is now suspicious of all catering companies. In any of these cases, you need to address the concern directly. Comments like these can start that conversation:

"Catering companies are difficult places to run."

"Let me tell you about a problem I had with a catering company recently."

"What would it take to renew your confidence in using catering companies?"

"Did the catering company that caused you the problem give you an adjustment?"

Competitors

The customer may be leaning towards using a specific competitor. You want to promote the benefits of your company, without resorting to slamming the other company. Again, this should be done only after the buyer uses the competitor against you in the discussion. Respond with a comment like this:

"It's very interesting that you've mentioned XYZ Catering. They are one of the better caterers in the area. In fact, I would say that they are probably one of our top three competitors. Some of my best clients use us regularly and also use XYZ Catering. As those customers explain it to me, they use XYZ Catering when less impact is required for the event, and they choose us when they want the food and service to be talked about by

their customers or guests in a special way. In other words, they rely on us to make them look great in front of their important guests."

It is very wise not to knock the competition without good reason. The only logical time to offer comparisons between yourself and another caterer is when a shopper brings the other caterer up by name. When a shopper says, "I'm also looking at XYZ Catering and they have much lower prices than you do," you might wish to launch the above script to make a valid comparison and to extend your sales conversation.

Postponing a decision

The customer may want to consult with someone else—or may say that in order to postpone having to make a decision. Respond to the customer's desire to talk it over with someone else with comments like these:

"That's a great idea; let me step out while you use my phone to call them."

"Let me arrange for you to use a desk in one of the conference rooms to make your calls."

"Great. Let's decide now what you want to ask them so that I can make sure that I've given you all of the answers that you require."

Handling difficult concerns

The customer may have strong objections or concerns about something, from price to comparison with competitors. You need to engage them in the response to their concerns:

"It's interesting that you've brought that up because many of my best clients made the same observation the first time they heard it. Let me take a moment and provide you with the same explanation that I gave to them, which convinced them to use our catering."

"Are you sure ... ?"

"Are you sure?" is a difficult script to say, but it is very powerful and creates a few moments for both the salesperson and the buyer to rethink what just happened and what is about to come.

Working with the frozen shopper

A "decision freeze" can be expected in most selling situations. In many cases, it comes up because the buyer can't find a reason to make a quick decision. The customer wants your catering, but you have to give a reason they need to buy it today.

This is a great time to remind your buyer of the advantages your catering holds for them — remind them that they need to make a quick decision because others are also looking to book for the same date. Creating urgency can help you overcome the "decision freeze."

"Sarah, it's natural for you to think about what you want to do before you make a decision. However, I'd like to suggest some important things to consider that might show you why postponing your decision might not be the best step to take."

"Ms. Weaver, I understand that deciding what caterer to use is a very big concern for you. The majority of my clients have had the same concerns that you now have. With your permission, I'd like to share with you what I've told other clients about what I call "decision freeze." In this way, you might get a better understanding of what others have done when they found themselves in the same situation that you now find yourself."

"Ms. Weaver, as I mentioned earlier, you are free to hold off your decision, but I need to make it clear that our ballroom may not be available much longer."

During a "decision freeze," you can help the buyer—and yourself—understand what the hesitation is all about. It's your job to make the buyer aware of their real concerns.

"Ms. Weaver, let's take a moment and discuss what some of your concerns might be. This way we both might be able to better understand what

information I need to give you so you can make a final decision."

As you listen to your buyer, be sure to note anything that might be considered positive. If they mention your "good food," that's positive. If they mention the beautiful new carpets in your banquet space, that's positive. If they mention your professional concern, that's positive.

Now take those positive thoughts and bring them back to the table. Get your buyer to realize that the opportunity to capture them for the guests (and for the buyer's peace of mind) is now.

Selling catering is selling handholding and the avoidance of embarrassment. It's selling your concern, love and skills to the buyer. Overcome "decision freeze" with your enthusiasm and by understanding the buyer's emotions.

TRANSITIONS

You've handled the customer's objections, gotten the information you need and given the customer the information they need about the benefits of using your catering. You're getting ready to close the sale, but you don't want to move too quickly. You don't want to close if the customer still has questions and isn't ready.

Gently controlling the selling pace

Phrases like these can help move the customer into the sense that they've already made a decision about using your company:

"This is a really interesting advantage ..."

"One of the real nice things about ..."

"Your guests will love the fact that ..."

"One of my customers made me realize that ..."

"What many of my clients find advantageous is ..."

 Pay attention to the body language and eye movement of the buyers. Are they nodding their heads in agreement with you as you speak? Are they sitting forward towards the action? Are they smiling to themselves or to each other? When you point to something with your pen, do they really look at it?

Presenting the menus

There are several ways to offer menus and their prices during a presentation. First, and most often used, is leading with a higher priced package to maximize the sale. If the shopper doesn't respond, the salesperson then shows a lower cost package. This system will work.

However, a far better method, referred to as the matrix, lets the salesperson show three price points at once, leaving no doubt that the salesperson is being customer-friendly and is not concerned with the amount of money that the shopper will spend. This will relaxe the shopper. Here is the script:

"Sarah and John, I would like to show you three very creative approaches to the menus and services for your event. Unlike other caterers, who tend to sell their most

expensive menus first, we wish our clients to know that no matter how much they spend with us they will get the finest quality and best service. Let's review the menus." [Salesperson places them out for shoppers to view all at once.]

"The first of the three [salesperson points to the middle menu from left to right] is our biggest selling menu this season and is priced in the middle at $55 per guest. The second [salesperson points] is our higher priced menu at $79 per guest. You may also choose our value menu [salesperson points] priced at $48 per guest. Which one would you like me to discuss in detail first?"

Most people will start with the middle menu and price. From a psychological point of view, it is the most comfortable place to start. Perhaps you can visualize how much easier and relaxing reviewing three menus is for the shopper than if they were given only one menu to review.

Postponing the menu

There sometimes are good reasons to help the client postpone making final decisions about the menu too far in advance of the event—including giving you a better opportunity to upsell menu choices as the event gets closer. Encourage the client to postpone a decision on the menu with scripts like these:

"Ms. Weaver, with respect to the menu selection, I've shown you a wide variety of successful menus and you seem to like many things that you've seen, but I'd like to suggest that we wait until the final 60 days before the party to make your final menu decision. That way, you'll be able to see the newest menus our chef has created and I can keep an eye out for special items that will add to your party's success."

"The reason I've spent so much time making you aware of so many of the different menus we have to offer is to give you the chance to either select your menu now or to wait until we get closer to the date of the event so we can include the newest and latest creations of our chef. By waiting a little bit, you can also take advantage of the best values."

"Sarah, many of my clients are postponing their final menu selections until 30 days before the event to insure that they are getting the most "in" foods. This might make sense for you—especially since your wedding isn't till next year and food fashion changes quickly. We simply lock in a price range and guarantee that price to you. Many of my clients look upon this as an advantage. Does this sound interesting to you?

Preparing for the close

These scripts can help you determine whether it's time to move into closing:

"At this point, are you willing to recommend our proposal for acceptance?"

"Shall I place a hold on May 25?"

"Should I call the florist to check on the availability of your choices?"

"Sarah, it appears that you really like what I've described so far; are we going to be your caterer for this very important wedding?"

"Our director of catering would like to meet with you. May I invite her in?"

"I'm interested to know how you liked our proposal. Was everything as you expected or do you still need some additional information?"

"Are you now willing to recommend us to the picnic committee for approval?"

"Is Thursday at 2 or Friday at 4 best for our next meeting?"

"With respect to your deposit, will you be using a check or a credit card?"

"Ms. Weaver, are we going to be your catering company of choice?"

CLOSING

Closing the sale is the moment of truth. It's the moment during a presentation when the salesperson culminates all his or her energy into getting a "yes" from the buyer.

Without a successful closing, both the buyer and the salesperson lose. Does this statement seem too strong? Well, let's think about it: If the buyer doesn't buy, then they will not get the benefit of your great food, service and overall hospitality. Also, if the buyer doesn't buy and the sale was built around proper profitability, you won't be as successful as you could have been. Thinking of it this way, both lose if the sale doesn't take place.

Closing techniques will vary depending on your buyer's needs at the time. Some buyers are easier to close than others. To be a successful closer of catering sales, you need to practice both on real buyers and when you are alone.

In simple terms, closing is just a collection of well-selected words infused with the salesperson's own enthusiasm and belief in the products and services. A well designed and performed closing gives the buyer permission to give you a deposit check.

Some things to remember

What do you think about closing? Is it uncomfortable or unnatural to you? Does your stomach churn when you know an opportunity to close is coming?

If you answered "yes" to these questions, you have the potential of becoming a super closer! Remember, Barbra Streisand gets nauseous when she performs. You may be thinking, "But she is performing, not selling." That's just what a good close is: a performance. It's a selection of well-chosen words, presented to the buyer using a well-written and rehearsed sales script.

Closing is not just an art; it's a science of procedures and techniques that help the buyer and you win! Practice your art and keep thinking about the science.

- Great closing techniques can make up for weak presentations and other shortcomings.

- Most salespeople are reluctant to ask for the order. They are afraid of the rejection.

- To be a great closer, be a great opener.

- Closing is a natural step that is part of the entire selling process; it is not separate.

- A salesperson needs an array of different closings to fit different types of buyers.

- The decision to buy is first made in the mind of the salesperson.

- Ask for the order several times during the sales situation.

- Keep your voice calm and low-key when doing a close.

- During a close, the salesperson should have the pen that the buyer will use to become a client in his or her hand at all times.

- A pleasant smile is a crucial part of closing.

The basics

Closing can happen at any time during a sale. In fact, a close can come before the sale actually begins.

"Sarah, before we begin, I'd like to ask if you've already decided to use our catering company, or are you also checking with other fine catering companies?"

Your own good judgment, based on the circumstances, must tell you when and how to move towards or into the close. In general, a close would be started when:

• You've finished your presentation.

• You've just completed a very strong point in your presentation.

- You've just overcome a strong objection from the buyer.

- The buyers indicate they are ready to buy.

Don't believe that there is only one perfect moment during the sale that the magical close needs to be offered.

What buyers want

Today, more than ever, buyers want value. This does not mean that they want cheap; they want value and performance for a fair price. Keep in mind some of what they may be thinking as you go into the close:

- Buyers are very suspicious about whether or not the salesperson is telling the truth; they often believe that salespeople are sneaky.

- Buyers often are convinced that catering companies will lower the prices if pushed a little.

- Buyers believe they can always find a catering company that will sell them what they think they want at the price that they want to pay.

- Most buyers consider the caterer to be less important to their event than the flowers and music. Because of this, they will tend to cut their budget on the food first.

- The buyer's desire to hire a caterer doesn't guarantee that they will actually do so. Wanting a service is not in itself reason enough to buy it.

Remember that buying catering is a tough task for shoppers. When they buy a car, they leave with the car. Once they give the catering salesperson a deposit check, they leave with nothing but the caterer's promise that the event will be successful. Why shouldn't they hesitate and be concerned?

Test closes

Is the time right to close? Statements like these let you test the customer's readiness to close:

"If you had to pick between these two linen colors, which one would it be?"

"Let's assume that I can get the starting time of the dinner changed as you wish; would that have a positive affect on your decision?"

"You seem to be comfortable with the service charges. Do you also feel comfortable with our deposit policy?"

"Let's assume for a moment that your financé wishes to move ahead; would you support him on this matter?"

"It sounds like you and I are in agreement with this—the menus and the price fit your budget. Am I reading this correctly?"

"Of the four menus, which is your favorite?"

The best thing to say after the buyer answers any of the above questions in a buying manner would be:

"That's great. Let me explain our deposit policy. We require $1,000 to hold your date and guarantee our services. Most clients use either a credit card or a check. Which would you wish to use: a check or a credit card?"

Styles

There are a number of styles you can use for closing. Some will work better with certain kinds of customers, and some will feel more natural to you. Experiment with different styles to see which you feel most comfortable with.

Offering choices:

"Do you want the order delivered at 11 or at noon?"

"Do you prefer copper or silver chafers?"

"Shall we start at 7 or 7:30?"

"It looks like it's come down to the beef or the grilled chicken menu. So, for your event on July 15, which do you prefer, the chicken or the beef?"

"Should we begin with a guarantee of 325 or 350?"

"Would you prefer the coat checkroom with an attendant or the self-serve coat racks?"

"We can use either the white or the black chairs. Which do you want me to reserve?"

Assuming the sale:

"It seems as if we've worked out all of the major concerns, haven't we?"

"It's settled then, we will have two bartenders. Correct?"

Recapping the information:

"Can we review for a moment why we're the best choice for your catered event? First, we can promise you creative menus. Second, we can provide incredible staff to make your guests happy. Third, our prices are fair for the fine level of quality you

*and your guests will receive. And fourth,
we really want to help you with this
event. I'd like to suggest that you make
the decision to let us be your caterer.
How do you feel about that?"*

Adjusting the deal:

*"If we lower the cost to you, will you say
"yes" today?"*

*"Let's assume that your husband likes
what we've talked about, will you let us
be your caterer?"*

*"Are you telling me that if we can lower
the number of staff for your event, you
will be able to purchase from us today?"*

Losing the date:

*"Sarah, it seldom happens in catering
companies, but we've been given a price
increase on meeting space, which takes
effect August 15. So I'd like to suggest
that we finish our arrangements so we
don't lose the value of a quick decision."*

"I'm concerned, Sarah, because June 20 is filling up very quickly. I'd hate to have you lose the opportunity to work with us. Why not make the decision right now to take advantage of our experience and beautiful property?"

Leading the way:

"I'm convinced we will do a great job for you. May I let my manager know you'll be booking with us for your meeting?"

Adding value:

"Ms. Weaver, if you are planning to have two more meetings over the next 12 months, you would qualify for our "best buyer" program, which gives a half-price rental fee for every third meeting. Would this be of interest to you?"

"As a first-time customer of ABC Catering, you qualify for an extra sleeping room night for your speaker. Will this help you decide to use us?"

Finding agreement:

"Do you like the banquet space I showed you?" (Yes.)

"Do you feel that the Asian menu would be liked by your guests?" (Yes.)

"Do you have confidence in our company?" (Yes.)

"Then it seems to me that we should move ahead with our paperwork."

Using testimonials:

"I understand that using a new catering company sometimes creates concerns. Let me share with you this wonderful letter from a new customer who, like you, had concerns about changing from her regular catering company. (Read the letter.) I'm confident that you also will write a letter to us about the excellent results you will receive by bringing your business to ABC."

Selling up to sell down:

"I suggest that we go with our Executive Continental Breakfast, which includes (list items) and is $9.75 per guest. Does that make sense to you?"(The buyers usually close themselves with something smaller.)

Closing assists:

"Do we have an agreement?"

"Can we have your okay on our agreement?"

"It's settled then. Can we get you signed up now?"

"Are you confident that we will do a great job on your event?"

The three tells

The sales process generally has three stages: Tell what you're going to tell. Tell your sales information. Tell what you've just told.

Tell what you're going to tell before you launch your presentation:

"Ms. Weaver, I wish to begin by taking a moment to tell you about what I'm going to cover during the next 40 minutes."

"First, I'll tell you about our owners and why they started ABC Catering. Then, I'll tell you about myself and the other ABC staff that will be assisting you in making your event one that all will agree is memorable."

"After this, I'll show you a variety of menus and I'll explain the different ways in which we can present the food to your

guests. If you wish, I'll even tell you what foods are most popular with our other customers this year."

"Next, we'll go over in great detail our prices and other costs, so you'll know exactly how much you will be spending."

"Then I'll explain how our deposit policy works and what you will want to do to reserve your date for the vent."

"Does this seem to be the kind of information you're looking for?"

Tell your sales information:

This "tell" is the simplest. During this part of the sale, you offer the customer all the information on your goods and services you need to get them ready for the close.

Tell what you've told:

When you realize you're about to finish with the second "tell," you need to get your mind ready to launch your first close. It's simply a rehash of the first "tell," and can take 2-3 minutes.

"Ms. Weaver, let me take a minute to review what we've covered so far. I've explained about our owners and staff. I've made you aware of the incredible menus that we have to offer you, and of some of our hottest themes. I've discussed some realistic prices and costs with you. It seems like you both like our Asian-themed buffets very much. All I have left to do is to make you aware of our deposit policy so you will be able to make a decision."

"It's quite simple: We ask that a customer provide us with a $500 deposit to reserve us for the requested date. Some use a check for the deposit; others use a credit card. Which would you like to use for your reservation deposit: a check or a credit card?"

 The three tells has helped countless new salespeople raise their closing averages because the client hears during the first part of the sales presentation that you will be explaining the prices and deposit policy at the end. By the buyer's own agreement, the salesperson now has permission to close the client.

Temporary hold

This technique is usually used in situations where the shopper has a lot of hesitation and is resisting making a buying decision. Letting the customer know that you have put a temporary hold on the date indicates that you're assuming the decision will be made soon.

"Mr. and Mrs. Nelson, the hour that we've spent together has proven to me that ABC Catering is right for your event. I'm also going to assume from your comments that you agree. I am, however, concerned with the date that you've chosen because it's a very busy one for us."

"I took the liberty of putting a temporary hold on our best event leader and six of her best assistants. I really wasn't supposed to do this, but I know how much your daughter's wedding means to

all of you and, quite frankly, I always want to have the absolutely best events that I can for my clients. The seven people that I've reserved as part of your event team will guarantee that your family and friends will talk about the wedding for years to come."

"Let me explain how I can place an official temporary hold on May 15 that will give you the time you need to make all of your final decisions. Is this going to help you?"

Rules of closing

There are a number of basic rules that help you close sales most effectively.

Questions keep control

Most professional salespersons agree that during a critical closing situation, the person who wants control needs to ask questions for the other person to answer.

You may ask, *"Ms. Weaver, would you prefer to use a credit card or a check?"*

If the buyer answers, "I'm not sure," the wrong response would be *"Use whichever one you prefer,"* because that's not a question. The better response would be, *"Do you get travel miles or bonus points when you use your credit card?"*

When the salesperson offers a non-question

like "Use whichever one you prefer," it gives the buyer an easy way to say something like "Well, let me check my bank statements at home and call you tomorrow." It makes it more likely that they can block you from completing the sale.

Don't talk at the wrong time

This may sound absolutely stupid, but once you ask your buyer for the order, the person who speaks first usually loses!

No talking! We mean it. Just 30 seconds of non-talking will seem like 100 years to even the senior sales staff, so this isn't easy.

If you must talk, it must be in the form of a question:

"Sarah, you've been rather quiet. I wonder, is your silence resulting from an error in my selection of menus or prices? Which is it, the menu or the price?"

This keeps you in control of the sales flow.

Don't forget to smile

Who wants to buy from an unfriendly salesperson? If you have a pleasant smile on your face while you're closing, you will win more sales and friends.

It's okay to temporarily stop the close if you need to

The most important thing about closing is to remember that starting it is the most difficult and the most important stage. Once you offer a close to the buyer, it's clear that you need to be taken seriously.

So it's okay to settle back in your chair and stop the close process, if that's what your instinct tells you to do. You might go back and answer some objections, or even to start selling again.

The point is, it's up to you to decide what you want to do next.

Leave the buyers alone

Often, a salesperson works long and hard to get the buyer to make a decision before leaving. But you need to sell smart as well as hard. Before they walk in, or open the door to you, most buyers promise themselves that they won't buy today, no matter what. They may even tell each other to be firm, just in case one of them weakens.

The only way you'll make a sale today with these buyers is to make an excuse to leave them alone, so they can mutually agree to break their promise to each other about not buying today. Go to the bathroom. Check with your secretary about something. Ask to be excused to call your spouse. Find a reason to leave the room.

Agree, then show leadership

Agreeing with an objection or concern shows that you understand the customer's concerns. But as the salesperson, you need to lead the customers to the correct decision.

"Sarah, I really agree with you that it will be less costly if you don't have the tent, but have you thought hard about what will happen if it does rain—especially during the meal? Here's how I see it ..."

Upselling

After the sale is complete your upselling begins. There is never a better time to sell more to a customer than immediately after they have just made the decision to buy. You can encourage the customer to purchase more of your services with scripts like these:

"Thank you for your order. May I show what we can do for just $500 more?"

"I am so excited about being selected to do your company picnic. Can we take a moment to talk about your upcoming December holiday party? If we can do both, I'm sure we can offer you some additional value on the two parties."

Guarantees

The guarantee of a certain number of guests the client must pay for is one of the sticking points for some customers. These scripts help you use the guarantee to close the sale:

"Ms. Weaver, let's take a moment so I can explain how our company deals with your guaranteed number of guests."

"You've mentioned, several times, that you are planning for 150 guests. One of the advantages of using our company is that we give you our "cushioned guarantee." The cushioned guarantee lets you worry less about whether or not all of your invited guests will be coming to the event. In your case, the cushion will be seven guests. This means that you will only be responsible for paying for 143 guests—or the actual

*number that come to the event, if it's
more than 143."*

*"The cushioned guarantee is one of the
reasons for our exciting growth as a caterer.
It just takes the pressure off our customers
for paying for guest who don't come. Don't
you agree that this is a great idea?"*

Another guarantee script:

*"So, Sarah, please let me explain how our
company handles the guest guarantee for
the wedding. As you both know, most
caterers require that the host and hostess
give them a final number of guests so the
caterer will know what to prepare and
charge for, whether all of these guests
come or not."*

*"At our company, we realize that when
inviting several hundred guests to a
wedding, even after they confirm by mail
that they are coming, a few often still
don't make it for reasons of health,
missed airplanes, etc."*

"We handle the guarantee differently than other caterers. We've made it more flexible and realistic for our clients. Let's say that you give us a final guarantee of 225 guests for the wedding. Even though we will be prepared to serve the full 225, we will permit you to have a leeway of five guests. This means that if only 220 guests come to the wedding, you would only be charged for the 220, not the original guarantee of 225 that you gave to us. We feel that this is a wiser way to treat our clients. Don't you think that our more liberal guarantee policy is an advantage for you?"

PROSPECTING

Great salespeople are always looking for ways to create more customers. But where do you find them? Sometimes it's through referrals from current customers, sometimes it's through sending out marketing materials, sometimes it's through cold-calling. Sometimes it just takes asking the people you meet on a daily basis. You can't make a catering sale until others know you are a caterer. I know of one successful caterer was who was stopped by a police officer for speeding and ended up selling him a wedding. That's prospecting!

Basics of telemarketing

When you're talking to someone over the phone, you can't use your smile and your gestures to help engage them, so your words and tone of voice need to carry the message. Remember:

- You need to be a good listener.

- Take notes as you talk with your contact.

- Stay on track.

- Concentrate on what you say, how you say it and the tone of your voice.

- Turn a negative response into a sales advantage.

- Never apologize for calling.

- Explain your offer in clear terms
  with, "What's In It For Me"?
  at the forefront.

- Write a script or checklist to follow
  during the call.

Asking for referrals

Referrals from current clients are great prospects because of the appearance of an endorsement by someone they know and respect. Satisfied customers won't always think to refer their friends and acquaintances to you; you have to ask for it.

"Who else do you think would like to learn about our fine catering? Thanks for the referral. May I use your name when I call them?"

"Thanks for the referral. Does she, like yourself, make the decisions about purchasing larger catering orders?"

"I know that you are well respected in your field; a referral from you could really help me. Is there anyone you know that I might call about our catering?"

Using a script to get in

Sometimes it seems like you just can't get past the person answering the phone. But you can't sell your services unless you get to the right person. This script can help you gently get through:

"Hello, this is Mary Stevens with ABC Catering. May I please speak with Mr. Thompson?"

Receptionist: I'm sorry Ms. Stevens, but Mr. Thompson is in a meeting. May I ask what this is in regards to?

"Then, may I please speak with Mr. Thompsons assistant?"

Call transferred to assistant:
Mr. Thompson's office.

"Hello, this is Mary Stevens with ABC Catering. May I please speak with Mr. Thompson?"

Assistant: I'm sorry Ms. Stevens, but Mr. Thompson is in a meeting. May I help you?

"Sure, one of my clients, Kyle Phillips of 123 Corporation, suggested that I call Mr. Thompson about our new "nutrition break" catering that has helped his company increase morale and profitability."

Assistant: Well, we could always use some better morale and profitability, but he is busy at the moment.

"I'll call back later in the week. Please tell him that Mr. Phillips has asked me to call him about our catering company."

Making friends with the administrative assistant

No one is more important than the administrative assistant of a potential corporate client. He or she can be the guard dog that keeps you from ever talking to the potential client, or can become your advocate. Don't forget your salesperson charm and good manners when you talk to the them.

"I'm sorry, I missed your name when you answered the phone. May I ask your name?"

Administrative Assistant:
My name is Tami Martin.

"Well, Tami, I assume that since you are answering Mr. Thompson's phone, you must be very much involved in

the selection of caterers for your
special events."

Administrative Assistant: Well, I do help Mr. Thompson make some of the decisions ... he's so busy!

"Tami, let me review quickly why I was
calling Mr. Thompson and then maybe
you can help me decide what we should
do next."

Scripts

These scripts help you invite the person you're prospecting into a conversation with you. Remember to make sure you are using words and phrases that let prospective clients understand what benefits they will get from your services.

"Hi, my name is Mary Stevens from ABC Catering on Mason Street. I was hoping to send some information about company picnics to your office. Can you help me by telling me who would be the best person to send our menus to?"

"I'm Mary Stevens from ABC Catering. A few days ago I mailed your office a copy of our new menu. I'd like to speak with the person who orders your catered functions. Who would

that be? Thank you. Is that person in now? May I have a brief moment of their time?"

"Hi, Mr. Thompson, you're talking with Mary Stevens, the sales manager of ABC Catering. As you will remember, I sent you our new menus last week. I'm calling to invite you and four others from your company to a special tasting luncheon I'm hosting for our best clients."

"Hello, I'm Mary Stevens of ABC Catering and I've been making appointments to visit growth companies to explain some new ideas we have on corporate entertaining. May I ask you a few questions?"

"Hello, this is Mary Stevens. I'm the sales manager with ABC Catering. If you recognize my name, I know that you received the letter I sent you recently about planning for your upcoming holiday party."

FINAL THOUGHTS

Think before you speak. Form a picture of the words in your mind and see them as they leave your mouth.

Sell based on what your catering does, not what your catering is.

Selling is simply stopping the buyer from going somewhere else to shop, while giving permission for the buyer to purchase from you today.

Never take "no" personally.

Failure to make a sale may make you feel unfulfilled—but not like a failure. Remember, you didn't sink the ship.

NOTES

NOTES

NOTES

NOTES

NOTES

NOTES

NOTES